Exploring World History

INDIA

Mason Crest
450 Parkway Drive, Suite D
Broomall, PA 19008
www.masoncrest.com

Printed and bound in the United States of America.
First printing

9 8 7 6 5 4 3 2 1

Series ISBN: 978-1-4222-3529-4
ISBN: 978-1-4222-3533-1
ebook ISBN: 978-1-4222-8353-0

Cataloging-in-Publication information from the Library of Congress is on file with the publisher.

On the Cover: The Taj Mahal, India's most famous site; independence leader Mahatma Gandhi; artwork from the Hindu tradition; a painting showing life in one of India's princely states.

Exploring World History

AFRICA
AUSTRALIA
CHINA
INDIA
JAPAN
LATIN AMERICA
NORTH AMERICA
POLAR REGIONS

Contents

A *priest from the Toda tribe who live in the Nilgiri Hills in south India.*

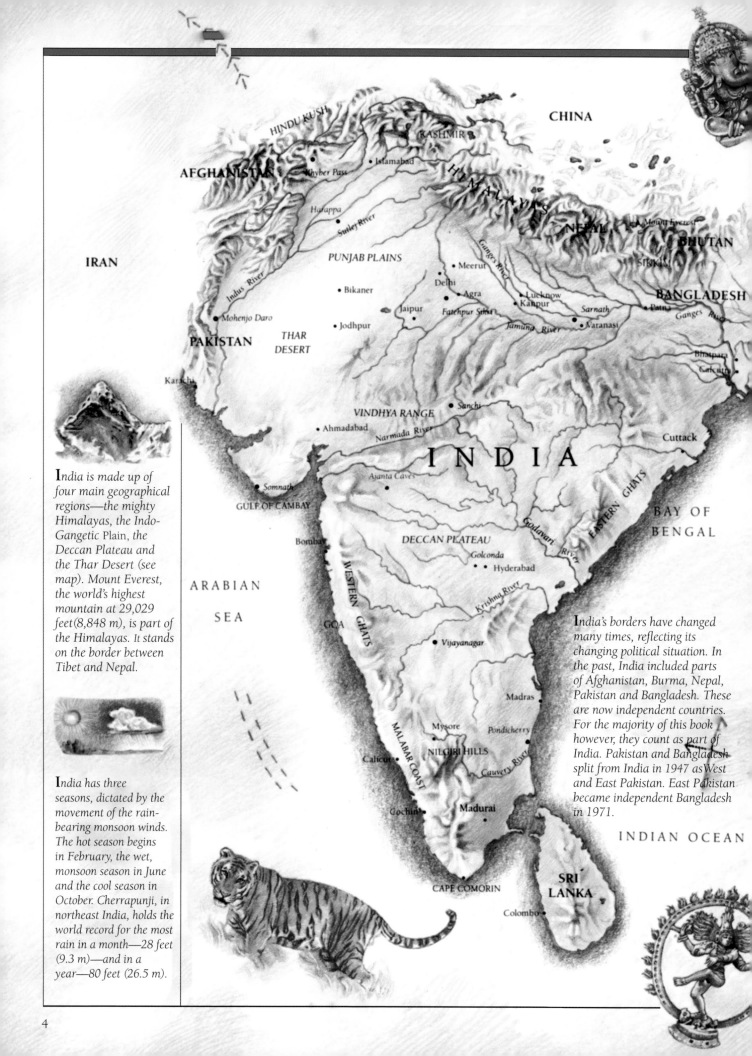

AFGHANISTAN

CHINA

HINDU KUSH

KASHMIR

• Islamabad

Khyber Pass

HIMALAYAS

NEPAL

Mount Everest

BHUTAN

IRAN

Harappa

Sutlej River

SIKKIM

Ganges River

BANGLADESH

PUNJAB PLAINS

• Meerut

• Bikaner

Delhi •

Lucknow

Sarnath

• Patna

Indus River

Jaipur

Agra

Kanpur

Ganges River

• Mohenjo Daro

• Jodhpur

Fatehpur Sikri

Jamuna River

• Varanasi

PAKISTAN

THAR
DESERT

Bhatpara

Karachi

Calcutta

Sanchi

VINDHYA RANGE

• Ahmadabad

Narmada River

INDIA

Cuttack

Ajanta Caves

India is made up of
four main geographical
regions—the mighty
Himalayas, the Indo-
Gangetic Plain, the
Deccan Plateau and
the Thar Desert (see
map). Mount Everest,
the world's highest
mountain at 29,029
feet (8,848 m), is part of
the Himalayas. It stands
on the border between
Tibet and Nepal.

• Somnath

GULF OF CAMBAY

Bombay

DECCAN PLATEAU

Godavari River

EASTERN GHATS

BAY OF
BENGAL

ARABIAN

SEA

WESTERN GHATS

• Golconda

• Hyderabad

Krishna River

GOA

India has three
seasons, dictated by the
movement of the rain-
bearing monsoon winds.
The hot season begins
in February, the wet,
monsoon season in June
and the cool season in
October. Cherrapunji, in
northeast India, holds the
world record for the most
rain in a month—28 feet
(9.3 m)—and in a
year—80 feet (26.5 m).

• Vijayanagar

Madras

Mysore •

Pondicherry

Calicut

NILGIRI HILLS

MALABAR COAST

Cauvery River

Cochin

Madurai

India's borders have changed
many times, reflecting its
changing political situation. In
the past, India included parts
of Afghanistan, Burma, Nepal,
Pakistan and Bangladesh. These
are now independent countries.
For the majority of this book
however, they count as part of
India. Pakistan and Bangladesh
split from India in 1947 as West
and East Pakistan. East Pakistan
became independent Bangladesh
in 1971.

INDIAN OCEAN

CAPE COMORIN

SRI
LANKA

Colombo •

1 Exploring India

The Story of India

What comes to mind when you think of India? The beautiful Taj Mahal (see page 31)? Huge elephants, ferocious tigers, shimmering peacocks and agile monkeys? Exotic plants like **banyan** trees, and mangroves? Cool cotton and spicy food? India is all these things and many others. Its sights, smells, sounds, wealth and poverty have fascinated visitors and explorers for thousands of years. The history of India's exploration is also a history of trading and invasion—from the Aryans (see pages 8-9) to the Mughals (see pages 26-31) to the British (see pages 36-41). Each power left its mark, adding to India's diversity.

Exploring People of Yesterday and Today

Very little is known about the first inhabitants of India. It is thought that two hundred to four hundred thousand years ago originally there were two distinct groups of peoples who spoke different languages and used tools either made of solid stone or flakes of stone. This indistinct period gave way to the great Indus Valley Civilization (3000 BCE) that lasted for four thousand years. Many different types, tribes and groups of people live in India today. Several of these tribal peoples, such as the Nagas of the northeastern hilltracts, have their own homelands within India.

Exploring This Book

This book is divided into six chapters. After this chapter on Ancient India there is a chapter that covers the Muslim invasion up until 1001. Chapter three looks at India under Muslim rule, while chapter four deals with the arrival of the first European travelers and traders. Chapter five explores India under British rule, with the final chapter looking at India today.

Vishnu the preserver, one of the major gods of the Hindu religion. Here he visits the Earth in the guise of a fish, to save mankind.

Religion in India

Three-quarters of all Indians are Hindus. They believe in a supreme being, called Brahman, whose various characters are represented by three main gods—Brahma (the creator), Vishnu (the preserver) and Shiva (the destroyer). There are thousands of other gods and goddesses. Some people worship in temples; others in small shrines at home. But Hinduism is an extremely flexible religion—some Hindus do not perform any formal worship. Hindus believe in **reincarnation.** For them, the ultimate goal is *moksha,* or salvation from the cycle of birth and rebirth.

Other major Indian religions include Islam (see page 19), Buddhism (see page 13) and Sikhism (see page 35).

The Indus Valley Civilization

The first, and greatest, civilization in Ancient India developed around the valley of the River Indus (now in Pakistan) in about 3000 BCE. By 2500 BCE it had reached the height of its power. The Indus Valley Civilization was larger than any other ancient empire, including those of Egypt and **Mesopotamia**. Its two great centers were the cities of Mohenjo-Daro and Harappa.

An artist's reconstruction of the city of Mohenjo-Daro.

City Planning

The Indus cities were built along careful plans. A city was divided into two parts—the lower town, where most people lived, and a fortified **citadel**, built on a raised brick platform. The streets of the lower town were laid out in a grid pattern, with wide main roads intersected by narrower side streets. Houses were built of mud bricks and many had courtyards. Each house had a bathroom and an efficient drainage system. The citadel was protected by a massive brick wall. It is thought to have been the city's religious and administrative center. In Mohenjo-Daro, the citadel also housed the Great Bath (see 1), used for religious rituals. Each city also had huge granaries (see 2) for storing precious supplies of grain.

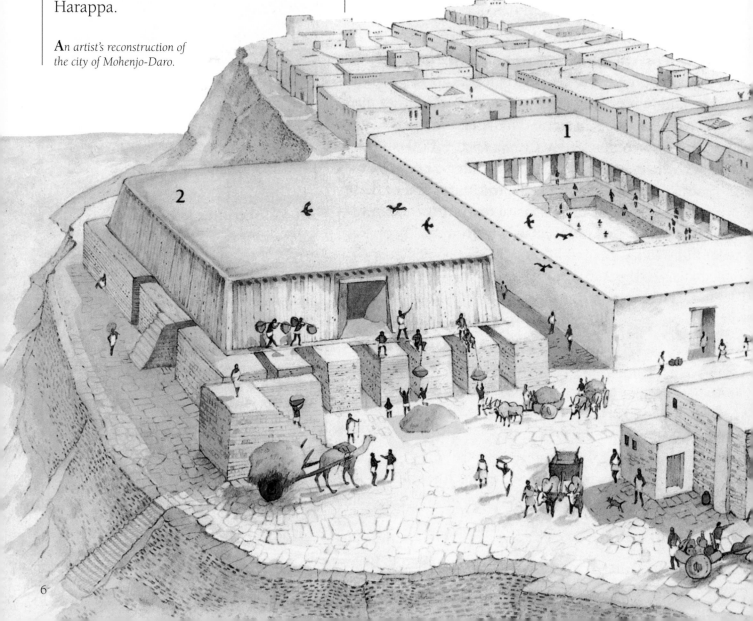

Indus Life

The Indus Valley Civilization had highly organized systems of trade and transport, with the cities as centers of commerce. Trade was based on agricultural produce, grown on the fertile river plains. The main crops were wheat, barley, dates and melons. People worked as farmers, merchants, potters, beadmakers, metal workers and so on. Many pottery figures have been found at the Indus sites. Some show gods and goddesses. Others are toys, such as bird-shaped whistles and cows with nodding heads. The Indus people loved jewellery and used tiny pottery animals as beads.

The Indus in Decline

In 2000 BCE, the Indus Valley Civilization collapsed. No one is sure why this happened. The cities may have been destroyed by frequent, terrible floods, or by the river changing course and causing the farmland to dry up. Another theory is that the Indus people overgrazed the land, leading to smaller harvests and a decrease in trade.

Sir Alexander Cunningham

Exploring the Past

Most of our knowledge of the Indus Valley Civilization and of Ancient India comes from archaeological finds. In the nineteenth century, the British **archaeologist**, Sir Alexander Cunningham, explored and **excavated** many ancient sites. He visited Harappa in 1853 and 1873. But the first real excavation of the Indus cities was begun in the 1920s and 30s by the Archaeological Survey of India, under another British archaeologist, Sir John Marshall. Marshall and his assistant R. D. Banerji found two previously unknown Indus sites dating back to the third millennium BCE.

*Among the most interesting **artifacts** found at the Indus sites, are small, carved stone seals. These were used by merchants to seal bundles of goods. Many of the seals show animals, such as one-horned bulls, elephants and tigers. Some show religious scenes. Each seal also had an inscription, proving that the Indus Valley Civilization had its own form of writing. Unfortunately, no one has yet been able to understand it.*

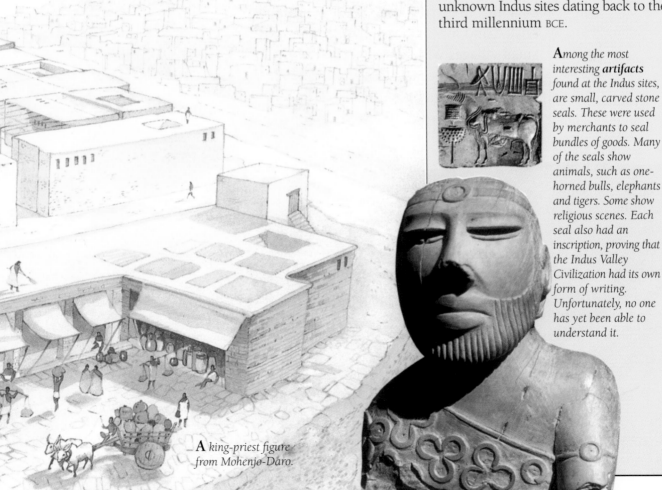

A *king-priest figure from Mohenjo-Daro.*

The Aryans Arrive

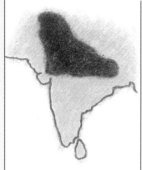

From *their arrival in India in about 1500 BCE, the Aryans spread southeast through the Indus Valley and down into the Ganges Valley (above).*

The *sixteen states of Aryan India in the sixth century BCE (above right).*

The *foothills of the Hindu Kush Mountains to the northwest of India, which now lie in modern-day Pakistan and Afghanistan.*

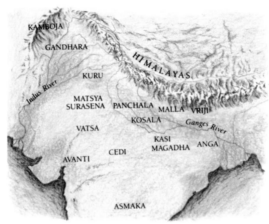

In about 1500 BCE, groups of **Indo-Europeans** traveled from Iran to northwest India. They became known as Aryans. They spread through the Indus Valley, then moved eastwards towards the Ganges Valley. The early Aryans roamed from place to place, searching out pasture for their herds of cattle. Gradually, they became more settled and formed themselves into small villages which grew into towns as the Aryans began to farm and develop their trading activities. The time of the Aryans is called the Vedic age.

The Aryans Explore

The Aryans were divided into various independent tribes, ruled by chiefs called *rajas* and by two councils—the *sabha* and the *sarniti.* The tribes gradually expanded their territories and began to trade, **bartering** for goods with cows and gold. With trade came increased prosperity. There were many conflicts between the tribes as they jostled for power. One famous battle, called the Battle of the Ten Kings, saw the victory of the Bharata tribe over an alliance often rival tribes. The modern name for India, *Bharat,* comes from this tribe. The famous Aryan epic, *Mahabharata,* is the story of rival cousins and their battles.

By the sixth century BCE, the tribes had grown into small kingdoms and **republics,** and the center of Aryan power had moved to the Ganges Valley. The rulers of the sixteen most powerful states—the *mahajanapadas*—struggled for control of the region. The kingdom of Magadha emerged as the victor. It controlled the valley and the main trade routes along the River Ganges for several centuries.

Indra, the Aryan god of war and the sky, mounted on his white battle elephant.

Aryan Religion

The Aryans worshiped many gods, especially those connected with nature and the world around them. Their most important god was Indra, god of the sky, rain, thunder and war. Other major gods included Varuna, controller of the universe, Surya, the sun god, Agni, the god of fire and Yama, the god of death. The Aryans offered sacrifices, often of animals, to the gods to gain their blessings. The priests who conducted the sacrifices and rituals were among the most important members of Aryan society. The offerings were placed in a sacred fire which carried them to the gods.

The mingling of ideas from the Aryan and Indus Valley religions formed the basis of Hinduism (see page 5).

The Rig Veda

One of our main sources of information about Aryan religion is a collection of 1,028 hymns, called the *Rig Veda*. These hymns were recited by the priests at sacrifices and ceremonies. Some hymns were addressed to specific gods. There were also battle hymns, observations and **dialogues.** The Aryans spoke **Sanskrit** and passed the hymns down by word of mouth. A hymn had to be spoken and pronounced absolutely perfectly for it to be effective. It was not until centuries later that the hymns were written down for the first time. The *Rig Veda* remains one of the most sacred Hindu holy texts and its hymns are still sung at weddings and funerals.

The Caste System

The class a person belonged to became important during Aryan times. These classes formed the basis of the caste system which still continues in India today. The three highest classes were the priests, called *Brahmins,* warriors and nobles, called *Kshatriyas,* and merchants, called *Vaishyas.* A fourth class, *Sudras,* was made up of the non-Aryan people who originally lived in the areas invaded by the Aryans. Sudras were usually farmers. The *Rig Veda* contains an account of how the caste system was created from a cosmic being, *Purusha.* The Brahmins came from his mouth, the Kshatriyas from his arms, the Vaishyas from his thighs and the Sudras from his feet.

Agni, the Aryan god of fire. The sacred fire was central to many Aryan religious ceremonies and rituals. It was thought that it linked Heaven and Earth, carrying people's sacrifices up to the gods.

The Greeks in India

During the sixth century BCE, the Persians (see map), moved into northwest India. The region of Gandhara became a part of the Persian Empire. A Greek doctor, Ktesias, who lived at the Persian court in the fifth century BCE, left an interesting, if inaccurate, account of life in northwest India. In it he describes a tiger as having three rows of teeth in each jaw and a sting at the tip of its tail which it shot at its enemy like an arrow!

Alexander and India

In 327 BCE, however, the Persians were overthrown by Alexander of Macedonia. Alexander came to the throne of Macedonia, in northeastern Greece, in 336 BCE, when he was just twenty years old. Within thirteen years he had conquered a vast empire which stretched from Greece through Egypt and Persia to India.

By 330 BCE, Alexander had defeated the Persians and their emperor, Darius. He now set out to reach the easternmost part of Darius's empire—in India. He fought his way through Bactria (see map), crossed the Hindu Kush (see map) and reached the River Indus in 326 BCE. At the battle of Hydaspes, he defeated the Punjabi king, Poros, and his troop of two hundred battle elephants. Alexander was so impressed by Poros's dignity and courage that he left him in charge of the Punjab. So far, the Indian campaign had been a success. But, on reaching the River Beas (see map), Alexander's army refused to go further and he was forced to turn back.

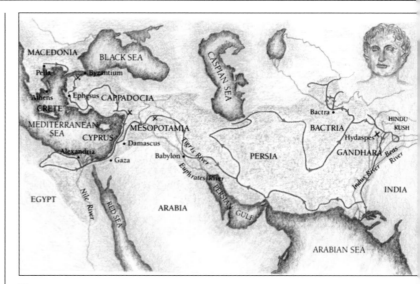

The map above shows Alexander's empire at its greatest extent.

Alexander's defeat of the Persians paved the way for his journey into India.

The Search for the "Ocean"

Alexander had heard many tales of India. Many Greek writers had portrayed India as a place of monsters, poisons, gold and gems. Reports had reached Greece of giant, gold-digging ants, wool growing on trees, men who lay on their backs and used their huge feet to shade them from the sun and elephants that could be trained to sew.

Alexander wanted to solve the mystery of the "Ocean." He had been taught that this was a huge, continuous sea which flowed in a circle around the land. He believed that if he crossed the River Indus, he would find the "Ocean." When he finally reached the Indian Ocean, he sacrificed some bulls to the Greek sea god, Poseidon, for leading him to his goal.

Alexander's quest to find the "Ocean" was fueled by fabulous, largely untrue, Greek accounts of India.

The Art of Gandhara

A lasting reminder of the Greeks in India is the influence of their artistic style on Indian art and sculpture. This was very strongly felt in Gandhara in the first and second centuries CE Greek and Buddhist (see page 13) styles of sculpture merged to produce graceful statues, draped in long, flowing robes. This was not the result of Alexander's legacy, however. Greek styles of art were copied by the Romans whose traders were in regular contact with India (see page 18).

The capital of the Mauryan Empire

The Rise of Chandragupta Maurya

In about 321 BCE, a young prince, Chandragupta Maurya, seized power and founded the great Mauryan Empire. He built his capital at Pataliputra (modern-day Patna). He defeated the Seleucid Greeks, who had inherited the eastern part of Alexander's empire, but remained on friendly terms with them. In about 305 BCE, the Seleucids sent an **envoy**, Megasthenes, to Chandragupta's court at Pataliputra. Megasthenes wrote a detailed account of his Indian experiences in a book called the *Indika*.

Megasthenes' book was important because it formed the Christian view of India right up until the Middle Ages (c.500-c.1500). In the *Indika*, Megasthenes describes the empire's administration, economy and secret service. Megasthenes also relates how Chandragupta lived in great luxury at Pataliputra, in a huge wooden palace. The Greek reports that Chandragupta lived in fear of his life and slept in a different bedroom every night to avoid being assassinated. Whenever he left the palace, he was guarded by a band of women on horseback. Chandragupta died in about 297 BCE.

2 India to 1001 CE

Reforms and New Religions

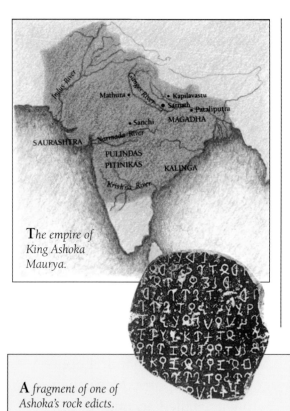

The empire of King Ashoka Maurya.

A fragment of one of Ashoka's rock edicts.

Under Ashoka, the grandson of Chandragupta, the Mauryan Empire reached the height of its power. Ashoka came to the throne in 269 BCE and became the greatest ruler of Ancient India. Because of his powerful personality most of India came under Mauryan rule.

The Kalinga Campaign

One of the few places in India which had resisted the Mauryans was Kalinga on the east coast (in modern-day Orissa). In 260 BCE, Ashoka launched a successful but ferocious campaign against Kalinga. According to Ashoka 100,000 people were killed in battle, many more died after and 150,000 were **deported.** Ashoka was filled with remorse. In an effort to make amends, he converted to the Buddhist religion which preaches non-violence (see box).

Ashoka's Edicts

Our main source of information about Ashoka and his reign is the collection of edicts (Qaws) and inscriptions which he had carved on rocks and sandstone pillars throughout his empire. These were deciphered for the first time in 1837 by a British **orientalist,** James Prinsep. Some were placed at the borders of the empire, showing its huge size. Others were located in places connected with the Buddha or along **pilgrimage** routes. The inscriptions begin with the words, *"The King, The Beloved of the Gods, Piyadassi, speaks thus…".* Some are accounts of Ashoka's conversion to Buddhism. Others are **proclamations** from Ashoka to the people. They explain his policy *of Dhamma* which stressed tolerance, respect for other people, social responsibility and non-violence. Special officers were appointed to travel throughout the land and explain Dhamma.

Thanks to the edicts, we now have a good picture of Ashoka's personality and reign. Before they were deciphered, very little was known about this great king.

Ashoka Explores his Kingdom

Ashoka traveled widely through the empire listening to people's opinions. This was highly unusual at a time when emperors were only really seen outside their palaces to go hunting or to go into battle. Ashoka tried to make people's lives easier, by building roads and rest houses, setting up free hospitals and veterinary clinics, bathing tanks, drinking places for cattle and planting shady trees.

Ashoka's famous Lion Capital can be seen on India's modern-day banknotes.

The Sarnath Lion Capital

The four-lion capital (sculpture on top of a column), which is a symbol of the modern republic of India, originally stood on top of one of Ashoka's finest pillars. It stood in the deer park at Sarnath, near Varanasi, where the Buddha preached his first sermon (called the Turning of the Wheel of Law). The four lions look in four directions, so that their roars reach the four corners of the Earth just as the Buddha's teachings do. Below them are four royal animals—the horse, bull, lion and elephant—and four wheels, representing the Buddha's teachings. The lions originally supported a huge wheel, the symbol of Buddhism.

A statue of the Buddha preaching at Sarnath.

The Teachings of the Buddha

The Buddha, or "**Enlightened** One," was born in about 560 BCE. His real name was Siddharta Gautama and he was the son of a king. Siddharta lived in the royal palace, surrounded by luxury. But he became more and more dissatisfied with life and, at the age of twenty-nine, decided to give up all his belongings, leave the palace and roam the world in search of truth. He found that the best path to follow to the truth was one of meditation, non-violence and moderation, and these elements form the basis of his teachings. The Buddha wandered throughout India for forty-four years, preaching his message. Buddhism had great appeal for ordinary people. It had no caste system (see box on page 9) so they did not feel downtrodden and the Buddha preached in the popular, local language, rather than Sanskrit, the language of the upper castes.

The Great Stupa (Buddhist shrine) at Sarnath.

The Glory of the Guptas

This map shows the probable extent of the Gupta Empire under King Chandra Gupta II.

Shiva the destroyer, one of the three major gods of Hinduism.

A carving of Vishnu sleeping on the coils of the many-headed serpent, Ananta. It comes from one of the earliest known Gupta temples in Central India and dates from about 425 CE.

Ashoka died in 231 BCE and the Mauryan Empire began to break up and finally collapsed in 184 BCE. For the next five hundred years, India was split into a number of small kingdoms and republics. Then, in about 320 CE, the second great Indian empire emerged in the Ganges Valley and Magadha—that of the Guptas. The first Gupta king, Chandra Gupta I, established himself by marrying into a respected royal family. Chandra Gupta I was succeeded by his son, Samudra Gupta. He was an active military campaigner, extending the empire during the forty years of his reign. In about 380 CE, Samudra was succeeded by his son, Chandra Gupta II, the greatest of the Gupta kings.

The Golden Age

The time of the Gupta Empire (c.320-550 CE) is often called the Classical Age of India. Under the **patronage** of the Guptas, literature, art, architecture and science flourished. Hinduism became the major religion of the empire, rather than Buddhism. Many temples were built with donations from wealthy families. Colleges were established for religious and formal education. Trade brought continuing prosperity. Textile making was one of the most important industries of the time, and large quantities of silk, cotton, **muslin** and linen were produced for export.

The Classical Age reached its peak during the reign of Chandra Gupta II (380-415 CE). The great Sanskrit poet, Kalidasa, is thought to have lived and written his poems and plays at Chandra Gupta's court. Kalidasa was described as one of the "nine gems" of the court. Sanskrit was encouraged as the language of the court and of the aristocracy. In the plays of the time, upper-class characters spoke Sanskrit, while lower-class characters and all women spoke Prakrit, the common language!

A gold coin from the reign of Kumara Gupta (415-455 CE) who was known as the Lion Slayer.

The direction of the Hun invasion.

The Hun Invasion

Chandra Gupta II was succeeded in 415 CE by his son, Kumara Gupta. During his reign (415-455 CE), the empire was threatened in the northwest by a Central Asian tribe called the Huns. Under the later Gupta kings, the empire gradually grew weaker as the Hun invasions became stronger. By the middle of the sixth century, it had broken up into several smaller kingdoms.

Achievements in Science

Indian science and mathematics were highly advanced by the time of the Guptas. A decimal system was already in use. Indian numerals later reached Europe via the Arabs and replaced Roman numerals. We still use them today. In the second century CE the oldest surviving Indian medical textbook was written. It was also a time of great discoveries in Indian astronomy. In about 499 CE, the astronomer, Aryabhata, proposed that the Earth was a sphere and spun on its axis. He also calculated the length of a year extremely accurately as 365.3586 days. At the time, his theories were rejected as being too revolutionary.

The Ajanta Paintings

The finest examples of Indian art from the Classical period are the paintings inside the Buddhist cave temples of Ajanta in West India. The caves were cut from solid rock, from about the second century onwards, but the paintings date from Gupta times. Only fragments from this period remain on the cave walls, mainly showing scenes from the life of Buddha. The artists prepared the rock surface with a coating of clay mixed with cow dung, straw and hair, covered with a smooth layer of white plaster. The painting was done while the wall was still damp. The caves were abandoned in the eighth century. They were rediscovered in the nineteenth century by British soldiers out hunting tigers. In the early 1920s, two Italian art experts began the task of restoring the paintings which had decayed because of pollution.

Chinese Explorers

Despite the **revival** of Hinduism during the Gupta period, Buddhism was still a major force in India. Buddhist **missionaries** from India traveled far and wide, spreading the word of the Buddha. In about 100 CE, Buddhism reached China. Chinese Buddhist monks wanted to learn more about their religion, their holy books, and to visit the places where the Buddha had lived and taught.

The Journey of Fa Hsien

Fa Hsien was born in China in about 370 CE. He became a Buddhist monk and decided to travel to India to bring back Buddhist texts, which he later translated from Sanskrit into Chinese. He set off on his journey in 399. To reach India, Fa Hsien had to cross the dreaded Takla Makan Desert (see map) following a trail of dead men's bones, avoiding bandits, and battling against the cold and his own tiredness. Then he crossed the Pamir Mountains and on through the Hindu Kush (see map). He described the mountains as sheltering *"dragons which, if once provoked, spit out their poison."* Once he reached India, Fa Hsien stayed at many Buddhist monasteries to study and debate with the monks. He also visited the Buddha's birthplace in Kapilavastu, the site of his enlightenment in Bodh Gaya and the site of his first sermon in Sarnath (see page 13). When he returned to China fifteen years later, he wrote a detailed account of his travels in his book, *The Memoirs of the Buddha's Dominions.*

Fa Hsien and Chandra Gupta II

Fa Hsien traveled around India during the reign of Chandra Gupta II. He reports that the empire was peaceful and prosperous. There was little crime and he was able to travel right across India without running into any trouble. He does not give many details about the emperor himself but says that the administration seemed mild and just. Fa Hsien also noted that most "respectable" people in India were vegetarians.

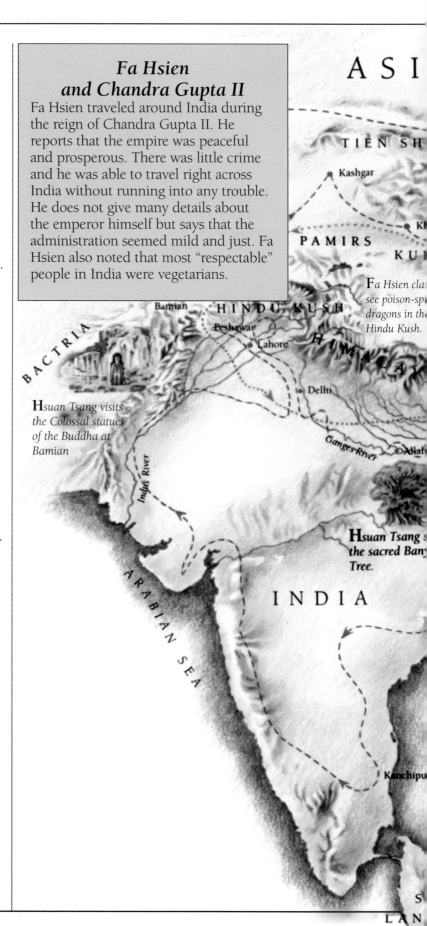

Fa Hsien claims to see poison-spitting dragons in the Hindu Kush.

Hsuan Tsang visits the Colossal statues of the Buddha at Bamian

Hsuan Tsang sees the sacred Banyan Tree.

Hsuan Tsang loses his way in the desert, is attacked by mid tribesmen but eventually comes to Hami.

Fa Hsien eventually returns to China after fifteen years, laden with religious objects and manuscripts

Fa Hsien crosses the Takla Makan Desert, following a trail of dead men's bones.

Hsuan Tsang sets out for India.

Hsuan Tsang stays at the Buddhist monastery of Nalanda.

Fa Hsien begins his journey in 399 CE.

Fa Hsien sails south to Sri Lanka.

BAY OF BENGAL

Hsuan Tsang found India a less peaceful place than Fa Hsien had. He was robbed by bandits twice and almost sacrificed to the goddess **Durga** by a band of robbers as he sailed down the River Ganges.

Fa Hsien returns to China stopping in Malaysia and Indonesia on the way.

The Journey of Hsuan Tsang

More than two hundred years later, in about 630, another Buddhist monk, Hsuan Tsang, set off from China to India. He had to leave China in secret, having been refused a travel permit by the emperor. His local guide abandoned him and he was forced to cross the desert alone on horseback. On the way, he was shot at by archers and lost both his water bag and his way. Things improved once he reached India. Hsuan Tsang visited many Buddhist sites and worshipped the **relics** of the Buddha. He also spent time at the great Buddhist monastery of Nalanda where he studied Sanskrit, philosophy and the Buddhist holy texts. Hsuan Tsang returned to China in 645, to a hero's welcome. The story goes that he needed twenty horses to carry back all the Buddhist manuscripts and statues he had collected. He spent the rest of his life translating the texts and writing his *Memoirs on Western Countries.*

Hsuan Tsang and Harsha

When Hsuan Tsang visited North India, it was mostly ruled by a king called Harsha. Hsuan Tsang greatly admired the king and spent a happy time at his court. He describes Harsha as being talented, generous, patient and energetic. Harsha traveled constantly around his kingdom, listening to people's comments and complaints. He also loved literature and even wrote three plays himself.

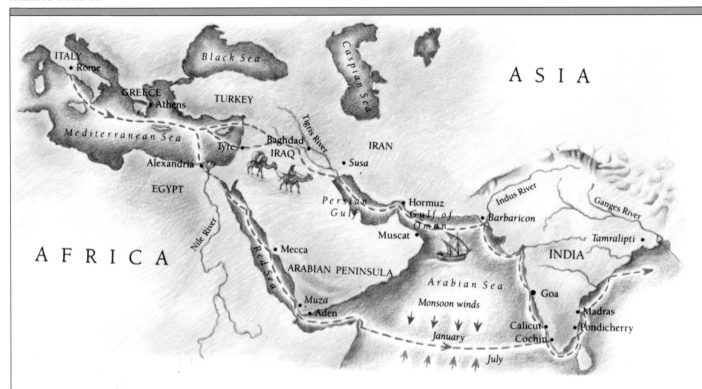

The map above shows the routes followed by early traders, overland and by sea, to India.

Early traders were dazzled by the variety and quality of goods they found in India, and by the colorful hustle and bustle of Indian life.

Early Traders

It was not just pilgrims and invaders who traveled to and from Ancient India. From very early on, traders' routes carried the fabulous goods of India to the West via the Middle East, the Mediterranean, China and Southeast Asia. Goods were carried both overland and by sea. India's spices, cotton, silk and precious stones were in great demand. The merchants of India enjoyed great wealth and became highly organized through guilds, called *shreni*.

Trade with Rome

During the first century CE, Indian trade with the mighty Roman Empire flourished. Wealthy Romans developed a taste for Indian spices, pepper and cloth. Live animals and birds were also in demand for the Roman emperors' wild beast shows. Thousands of tigers, lions and elephants were exported from India to Rome, together with peacocks and parrots as pets. Rome paid for these goods in gold. Roman coins have been found all over India, especially in the south near the main trading stations. There are also lists of Indian ports in a document called the *Periplus Maris Erythraei* (*The Periplus of the Erythraeum Sea*) which is thought to have been written in the first century. The *Periplus* also lists India's major exports—pearls, ivory, silk, pepper, textiles, precious stones and **tortoiseshell.**

A traditional Arab ship carrying merchants on a trading mission.

Sea Trade and the Arabs

Arab merchants had traded with India for hundreds of years before the Romans. The discovery of the **monsoon** winds in the first century BCE meant that ships could take a direct route across the Arabian Sea to the Persian Gulf and the Red Sea rather than following the slower route along the coast. One of the most important ports for the spice trade with both the Arabs and Romans was Malabar on the west coast. The decline of the Roman Empire in the fourth century CE gave a boost to Arab trade with India and they were soon in control of the main trading routes. The Arabs traded for horses, foodstuffs and metals. They also learned and exported Indian rice and sugar-cane growing techniques.

Sailors of all centuries have used the monsoon winds to guide them. The winds could be very treacherous.

Regions and Cultures

In the seventh century India split into independent kingdoms and states, each with its own distinctive identity, culture and language. Sanskrit was still used, but for courtly and official purposes rather than everyday speech and popular literature. Instead, local languages such as Tamil, Gujarati, Bengali and Marathi grew in importance.

The Spread of Islam

The religion of Islam was founded in Arabia in 622 CE by the Prophet Muhammad. It quickly spread throughout Arabia and North Africa. In 711, the Arabs conquered Sind, the region around the Indus **Delta** and brought Islam to India. Today, more than a tenth of Indians are Muslims and there have been violent clashes between the Hindu and Muslim communities in modern-day India. But the arrival of Islam in India was peaceful. The Muslims did not try to convert people by force but gave Hindus special status as a protected people.

3 India Under the Muslims

Muslim Invaders and Explorers

Mahmud of Ghazni

Although the Arabs had conquered Sind in the eighth century, the first real Muslim invasion of India began in 1001. The Turk, Mahmud of Ghazni, led bands of raiders from Afghanistan into northwest India almost yearly for the next twenty-five years. His aim was to plunder the wealth of the Hindu temples. He stole huge amounts of money, jewelery and gold and ruthlessly destroyed many temples in the name of Islam. In 1024, he attacked the temple town of Somnath in Gujarat. The temple contained an image which was worshiped by *"a thousand Brahmins continuously and washed every night in the River Ganges."* Mahmud ordered the image to be smashed and its coverings of jewels, gold and embroidered cloth to be carried back to Afghanistan.

The Delhi Sultanate

Mahmud of Ghazni died in 1030 and his place was taken by another group of Turks, under their leader, Muhammud of Ghur. By 1185, the Ghurids had control of northwest India. In 1193, they conquered Delhi which became their headquarters. Muhammud of Ghur was assassinated in 1206 and his general, Qutb-ud-Din Aibak became the first Sultan of Delhi.

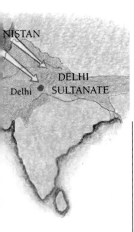

Within twenty years, the Sultanate had most of the Ganges Valley under its control Aibak was a former slave and the founder of the so-called **Slave Dynasty.** Aibak was succeeded by lltutmish who ruled from 1211-1236 (see box). By 1236, the Delhi Sultanate was firmly established as the greatest power in northern India.

Dynasties and Decline

The Sultanate had thirty-five rulers from several different dynasties from its beginnings to its decline in the sixteenth century. From the end of the fourteenth century, however, the Sultanate began to decline. Territory was lost and there were arguments about who should rule. Some Muslim nobles and Hindu chiefs broke away and declared their independence. In 1398, the Sultanate was attacked by the Central Asian chieftain, Timur. This weakened it further and it gradually shrank in size and importance. In 1526, at the Battle of Panipat, the last Delhi Sultan, Ibrahim, was defeated by a descendant of Timur, called Babur who was ruler of Kabul in Afghanistan. The Mughal Empire had begun (see pages 26-31).

Timur invaded and sacked the city of Delhi in 1398, dealing a bitter blow to the Delhi Sultanate (above).

Timur's raids were bloody affairs (left).

A European engraving of Timur of l826 (below).

Raziya Sultana

One of the most extraordinary rulers of Delhi was Raziya, the daughter of lltutmish. Her father was a wise, tolerant leader who groomed his daughter to succeed him. Raziya reigned for a short time, from 1236-1240, as the first woman ruler in the Muslim world. But many of the Sultanate's advisers and nobles resented having a woman on the throne and plotted her downfall and murder. She was, however, a firm and capable ruler. A historian of the time wrote that she was, *"wise, just, and generous,"* and *"endowed with all the qualities befitting a king!"*

The Qutb Minar (above) near Delhi is a tall victory tower built by Qutb-ud-Din Aibak in 1193. It was constructed to celebrate the first Muslim victories over the Hindus which marked the start of the Delhi Sultanate. The tower is over 200 feet (70 m) high. It has five tiers made of sandstone and marble, each with a balcony. Qutb-ud-Din only saw the tower reach its first story; the rest was completed by his successors.

Travelers' Tales

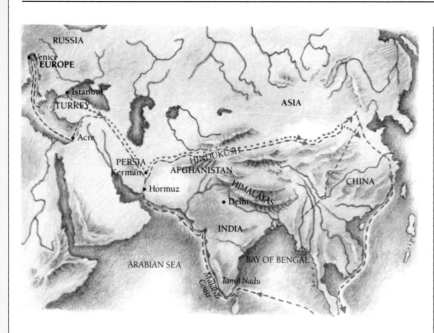

Marco Polo (1254-1324 CE) dressed in Tartar costume (right).

A map of Marco Polo's travels (left).

Marco Polo and his father and uncle leaving Venice for China in 1271 (below). From a French manuscript c.1400.

Apart from the Muslims, there were other foreign visitors to India during the thirteenth and fourteenth centuries. Their eyewitness accounts of events have been extremely valuable in piecing together a picture of Indian life during the early part of the Muslims' rule. Two of the most famous of these travelers were the Italian, Marco Polo, and the Moroccan, Ibn Battuta.

Marco Polo

Marco Polo was born in 1254 in Venice, Italy. At that time Venice was a great commercial center. Marco's family were wealthy merchants and made several journeys to the Middle East and Asia in search of trading opportunities. In 1271 Marco joined his father and uncle on their travels. They traveled overland, with the court of the great **Kublai Khan** in China as their final destination. Their journey took them through Turkey, Persia and Afghanistan, crossing into India through the Hindu Kush to join the **Old Silk Road**. The Polos spent seventeen years in China. On their return journey to Venice, Marco traveled up the west and east coasts of India and visited Tamil Nadu in southern India. In his book, *The Travels of Marco Polo,* he comments on the thriving trade in horses brought from Arabia.

Marco Polo died in 1324 after an adventurous life that inspired many explorers such as Christopher Columbus.

Early Europeans

During the fifteenth and sixteenth centuries, another group of people began to arrive in India. They were Europeans who came to trade rather than to travel. They had heard stories of the great wealth of the East and were unhappy that the Arabs were controlling its trade and its profits. To take advantage, the Europeans needed to cut out the Arab **middlemen** and trade directly with Asia. The first European country to make its mark on India was Portugal. By the end of the fifteenth century, the Portuguese had found a direct sea route to India and established trading posts on the west coast of which Goa was the most important (see pages 32-33).

Ibn Battuta, the Traveler of Islam, traveled three times further than Marco Polo.

Ibn Battuta

Ibn Battuta, known as The Traveler of Islam, was born in Tangier, Morocco, in 1304. In 1325, at the age of twenty-one, he left Morocco on a pilgrimage to Mecca the holy city of the Muslims. This was the start of a life of traveling in which he covered an amazing 75,000 miles (120,000 km) and visited almost every Muslim country, together with Southeast Asia and China. His only rule was never to travel the same road twice. In 1332, Ibn Battuta decided to visit India and try his luck at the court of the Sultan of Delhi, Muhammad Ibn Tughluq. He arrived in 1333, after a grueling and dangerous journey. Then he made his way to the Sultan's court, with his train of servants, wives and gifts of horses, camels and slaves for the Sultan.

Ibn Battuta was well received by Muhammad and appointed to the office of judge. In his book, the *Travels*, he describes Delhi as "*a vast and magnificent city, uniting beauty with strength*" and the Sultan as "*of all men the fondest of making gifts and of shedding blood.*" In 1354, Ibn Battuta returned to Morocco and dictated his account of his travels. He died in 1369 at the age of sixty-four.

South India Through the Eyes of Travelers

The two great independent kingdoms of South India – the Hindu kingdom of Vijayanagar and the Muslim Bahmani kingdom.

In the thirteenth and fourteenth centuries, southern India was raided many times by the Khalji and Tughluq sultans of Delhi. Their attempts to subdue the south were unsuccessful and led, in the middle of the fourteenth century, to the formation of two independent southern kingdoms—the Muslim Bahmani kingdom and the Hindu kingdom of Vijayanagar. The dividing line between the two was the Krishna River and the history of both kingdoms is dominated by their long-running battles over this fertile area.

Camel caravans were the usual form of transport for goods throughout India.

Athanasius Nikitin

Athanasius Nikitin set off from his home in Russia on a commercial visit to India in 1468. He spent four years at the rival Muslim-ruled Bahmani capital of Bidar. He was the only European to have visited it at that time. He describes it as the chief city of Muslim India but comments on the contrast between rich and poor Bahmanis, *"People … in the country are very miserable, whilst the nobles are very **opulent** and delight in luxury."* He says the nobles were carried from place to place *"on their silver bed,"* accompanied by horsemen, foot soldiers and musicians. Nikitin died before he could return to Russia. Fortunately, his account of his travels and experiences was carried safely to Moscow by some merchants in 1475.

What the Merchants Saw in Vijayanagar

The Hindu kingdom of Vijayanagar ruled over the far south of India for more than two hundred years. It was founded in 1336 by two brothers, Harihara and Bukka, and reached its peak under King Krishna Deva Raya who ruled from 1509-1530. He further expanded the kingdom and encouraged lucrative trade with Portuguese merchants and travelers. Gold, silver, horses, and Ceylonese elephants were imported into Vijayanagar. Rice, sandal wood, cloves and dyes were the major exports. Many of the Portuguese visitors commented on Vijayanagar's splendor and prosperity. Its huge citadel was surrounded by rings of fortifications and guarded by a large army. It had beautiful palaces, lavishly decorated temples and wide streets. Duarte Barbosa wrote in 1518, *"Among the most prized of the royal possessions are the elephants and horses, the king usually possessing more than nine hundred elephants and twenty thousand horses."* The King himself was described by a Portuguese traveler as *"the most feared and perfect king that could possibly be, cheerful … and very merry. He is a great ruler and a man of much justice."*

The End of the Empire

By the middle of the sixteenth century Vijayanagar's power had begun to decline. The Hindu kingdom had so far resisted the Muslims but, in 1565, it was defeated by neighboring Muslim sultans at the Battle of Talikota. Much of the city that had been described by the Portuguese traveler, Castantheda in 1552, as *"The greatest known to the whole world"* was destroyed.

This modern-day stall-holder in Mysore (South India) is trading in a market virtually unchanged since the fourteenth century. The snacks he is selling give some idea of the variety of food that has always been eaten in India.

Nicolo de' Conti

The Italian, Nicolo de' Conti, visited Vijayanagar in the early fifteenth century. He reports that the city was 60 miles (100 km) around and had a population of at least 90,000. He also writes that the King had 12,000 wives *"of whom 4,000 follow him on foot wherever he goes"* and *"a like number… ride on horseback."* The rest were carried in **litters.** De' Conti witnessed some of the many wars between Bahmani and Vijayanagar. He also describes the rite of *sati* where a Hindu wife is required to throw herself on her dead husband's **funeral pyre** (sati was banned in 1829). De' Conti began his travels to Asia in 1419. He did not return to his home in Venice until twenty-five years later, in 1444.

The Mughal Empire

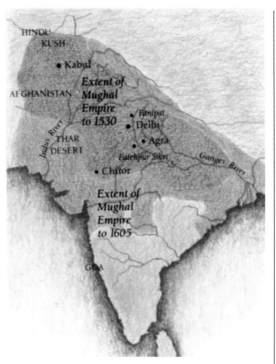

The extent of Mughal power by about 1605.

The first Great Mughal, Babur.

During the sixteenth century, much of India came under the control of another group of Muslims from the northwest—the mighty Mughals. They succeeded in establishing one of the most powerful and splendid empires ever seen, famous for the grandeur of its courts, buildings, gardens, art and literature. They were also famous for their six strongest rulers, known as the Great Mughals. These rulers started to explore India in detail and devised brilliant systems of communication and administration in order to rule. When the British came along two hundred years later they took over many of the Mughal systems of government.

Babur

The first Great Mughal, and the founder of the dynasty, was Babur who ruled from 1526-1530. In 1526, Babur marched from his capital in Kabul, Afghanistan, into India and defeated the last Sultan of Delhi, Ibrahim, at the battle of Panipat (see page 21). This gave him control of Delhi and Agra, which became the twin capitals of his empire. Babur was a fantastic general. By the time he reached India, he had fought against Turkish, Afghan and Persian forces. He studied his enemies' tactics and formed them into one, highly successful strategy. Even his greatest efforts, however, were no match for the Hindu Rajput warriors who defeated him in 1527.

Humayun

Babur's son, Humayun, was unable to defeat the Afghan forces of Sher Shah. In 1540 Humayun fled to Persia but the Mughals later defeated the Afghans and Humayun returned to India in 1555. Unfortunately, he died in 1556 before he could win back all of his lost lands.

Akbar the Great

The greatest Mughal emperor of all ruled a court that was larger and richer than that of Elizabeth I of England (who ruled at the same time as him). Akbar was the grandson of Babur and came to the throne at the age of fourteen. Akbar's reign lasted for forty-nine years, from 1556-1605. He strengthened the empire and reconquered the lands lost by his father. Akbar also won back the loyalty of the nobles. Just as importantly, he gained the allegiance of the powerful Rajputs by marrying a Rajput princess.

Akbar realized that the Muslim Mughals could only rule India successfully if they involved the Hindus and other non-Muslims. He banned the hated tax imposed on non-Muslims and on Hindu pilgrims and employed many Hindus in his administration.

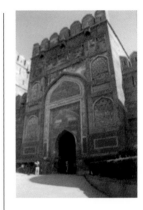

The magnificent fort in Agra dates from the sixteenth and seventeenth centuries when Agra was the capital of India.

Akbar loved riding and playing polo. He was a skilful swordsman and a good shot.

Fatehpur Sikri

In 1570, work began on the building of Akbar's new capital city, Fatehpur Sikri, to the west of Agra. Legend says that it was here that a Muslim holy man, Shaikh Salim Chisti, foretold the birth of Akbar's three sons. The prophecy came true. Filled with gratitude, Akbar had a beautiful sandstone city built and moved his court from Agra. But Fatehpur Sikri was abandoned after just fourteen years, probably because of problems with the water supply. Many of its amazing buildings still survive, including Shaikh Salim Chisti's tomb.

Two views of Fatehpur Sikri today, and a painting from Akbar's Memoirs showing the city being built.

A *Mughal painting of a Jesuit priest.*

What the Jesuits Saw

Among the Christians who visited Akbar's court were **Jesuit** missionaries from the Portuguese colony at Goa. Three Jesuit fathers arrived at Fatehpur Sikri in February 1580 and were made very welcome. Akbar even built them a chapel inside his palace. The Jesuits were disappointed, however, in their attempts to convert Akbar to Christianity. Other Jesuits followed. In their accounts, they describe Akbar as a man of *"medium stature, and strongly built. He wore a turban on his head, and the fabric of his costume was interwoven with gold thread.... On his brow he wore several rows of pearls or precious stone."*

A young Mughal prince visiting some Hindu monks as part of Akbar's policy of religious tolerance.

Exploring India's Religions

Akbar had a deep interest in religion. He summoned Muslim, Hindu, **Parsi**, Jain, Christian and Jewish scholars to his court and spent many hours talking to them about their religious beliefs. Akbar amassed a large library of religious books of all types. In 1582, he announced the formation of his own new religion, the *Din-i-Ilahi,* or Religion of God. Akbar brought together the best from all the religions he had studied.

Akbar died in October 1605. Like his father and grandfather, he left a detailed history of his life, the *Akbar-nama,* recorded by his **chronicler,** Abul Fazl.

Akbar's hardest campaigns were against the Hindu Rajputs. He captured the great Rajput fortress of Chittorgarh (below) in Rajasthan in 1568. He later formed an invaluable alliance with the Rajputs.

Jahangir embracing Shah Abbas of Persia (c.1620).

Jahangir

Jahangir followed his father, Akbar, on to the Mughal throne and reigned from 1605-1627. The seventeenth century was the golden age of the Mughals. They had luxurious palaces built, sat on jewel-encrusted thrones and surrounded themselves with finery. European visitors to the Mughal court were greatly impressed by its wealth and spectacle.

Jahangir followed his father's policies of treating both Muslims and Hindus with equal respect. Jahangir loved art and nature. His memoirs include many descriptions of unusual birds and animals illustrated by court painters. He had a reputation for cruelty and drunkenness, as well as for gentleness and charm.

In 1611, Jahangir married Nur Jahan, the Light of the World. She became one of the main sources of power behind the throne, raising her family and her favorite, Shah Jahan, to high positions in the court. When Jahangir died in 1627, Shah Jahan was crowned emperor.

Sir Thomas Roe (1581-1644)

Thomas Roe at Jahangir's Cour

England's first ambassador to India, Sir Thomas Roe, spent four years at Jahangir's court, from 1615-1619. He had been sent by King James I to seek a trade treaty from the emperor. He wrote an account of his life at the court and his experiences of Jahangir himself. Among many other details, he describes the strange ceremony which took place on the emperor's birthday. Jahangir sat on a set of golden scales and was weighed against sacks of gold and precious stones. These were later shared out among the people.

Jahangir weighing his son Prince Khurram (later Shahjahan) against gold on his birthday in 1607. From The Memoirs of Jahangir c. 1615.

A Mughal painting of Shah Jahan and his wife, Mumtaz Mahal.

Shah Jahan

Shah Jahan reigned from 1627-1658. He is best remembered for the great buildings which he commissioned, such as the Red Fort in Delhi, the Agra Fort and, of course, the Taj Mahal (see page 31). This was built as a memorial for Shah Jahan's wife, Mumtaz Mahal, the "Chosen One of the Palace," whom he married in 1612. Her sudden death in 1631, after the birth of her fourteenth child, left Shah Jahan devastated by grief. He spent two years in mourning. After Mumtaz Mahal's death, Shah Jahan left the business of wars and campaigns to his sons and devoted himself to his great passion for architecture. He also loved jewels and gemstones. His throne was the famous and fabulous "Peacock Throne." The canopy over the throne was held up by twelve emerald pillars. At the top of the pillars were two peacocks standing on either side of a tree, inlaid with rubies, emeralds, pearls and diamonds.

In 1658, Shah Jahan fell ill. His third son, Aurangzeb killed his older brothers, imprisoned his father in Agra Fort and declared himself emperor. Shah Jahan died in 1666.

The Red Fort in Delhi was begun by Shah Jahan in 1638 and finished some ten years later. The fort is built from massive blocks of red sandstone.

Aurangzeb receiving the head of one of his brothers, his main rivals to the throne, on a plate. When Aurangzeb came to the Mughal throne he called himself Alamgir –World Conqueror.

Aurangzeb

Under Aurangzeb, the last of the Great Mughals, the Mughal Empire reached its greatest size. But Aurangzeb's reign also heralded the beginning of the end for the Mughals. Aurangzeb ignored Akbar's policy of **religious tolerance** and equality. His narrow-minded belief in Islam lost him peoples' trust and resulted in many rebellions against his rule, including those by the Sikhs (see page 35), the Rajputs and the Marathas (see page 35). Aurangzeb reintroduced the tax on non-Muslims and ruthlessly destroyed many Hindu temples, often building **mosques** on top of the ruins.

Aurangzeb died in 1707. Soon afterwards the Mughal Empire began to disintegrate, weakened by invasions and in-fighting. There were emperors in place until 1857, but they ruled in name only. In 1858, the British sent the King of Delhi into exile.

The Taj Mahal

The Taj Mahal stands on the west bank of the Yamuna River near Agra. Shah Jahan summoned architects and craftsmen from all over the Mughal Empire and beyond to build this tomb for Mumtaz Mahal. He wanted it to be the most beautiful building ever created. Various designs were submitted to him and each was tried out as a wooden working model. The final design was probably a mixture of these ideas and Shah Jahan's own ideas. Building began in 1632 and took about twenty years to complete. The Taj Mahal is built of white marble and was originally decorated with precious stones. Inside are the tombs of Mumtaz Mahal and Shah Jahan. Legend has it that Shah Jahan intended building a black marble replica of the Taj Mahal on the opposite bank of the river, as his own tomb, but he was imprisoned by Aurangzeb before he could put his plan into action.

4 The European Presence in India

European Traders

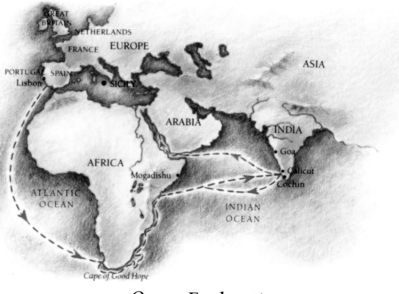

Vasco da Gama was born in 1460 into a military family. Discipline was the hallmark of his leadership. He died in Cochin in 1524.

Ocean Exploration

In July 1497, the Portuguese navigator, Vasco da Gama, led an expedition of four ships and one hundred and seventy men out of Lisbon harbor at the start of an historic journey. He sailed round the Cape of Good Hope, up the east coast of Africa and across the Indian Ocean. In May 1498, he reached the port of Calicut on the west coast of India and became the first European to reach India by sea.

Dutch trading ships of 1640.

Wealthy Portuguese traders enjoyed a privileged lifestyle. Here a merchant is being greeted by his Indian household and servants.

Da Gama was given a lukewarm welcome by the Hindu ruler of Calicut who dismissed the goods he had brought with him as cheap trinkets. The Muslim merchants were none too pleased to see the Portuguese either. Da Gama did manage to load his ships up with precious spices, however. In fact, he made enough profit from his cargo to cover his expedition expenses thirty times over.

More Portuguese Follow

A second Portuguese expedition sailed for India in 1500, led by Pedro Alvares Cabral. Cabral set up a trading post, or factory, at Cochin. Da Gama led a third expedition in 1502. Both of these expeditions used force to squash any opposition. For the next hundred years, the Portuguese controlled the trade in the Indian Ocean from their base at Goa on the west coast of India.

Trading Wars

Towards the end of the sixteenth century, Portuguese control of India began to weaken. By the early 1600s, Dutch and British merchants had set up their own rival East India companies to trade in India and Southeast Asia. The Dutch had the upper hand in the spice trade of Southeast Asia. The British, therefore, fixed their sights firmly on India. They set up their first trading post at Surat in 1612. By the late seventeenth century, their main rivals in India were the French who had established their own trading company in 1664 and their first trading post at Pondicherry. By 1690, the British had also settled in Madras, Bombay and Calcutta. Throughout the eighteenth century, the British and French fought for trading supremacy, with the British finally emerging as the victors.

The English East India Company

The English East India Company was set up in 1600 to trade with India and Southeast Asia. At first, the Company was solely concerned with the spice trade. But then the Mughal Emperor Jahangir allowed it to deal in silk and cotton, **indigo** and so on within certain parts of India as a reward for protecting Muslim pilgrims from Portuguese raiders as they traveled to the holy city of Mecca. These exotic materials quickly became a part of life for wealthy people back in Britain.

As Mughal power weakened (1666-1707), the Company seized any opportunity to control India and its trade. The English East India Company eventually formed the basis of the British Raj (rule) in India (see pages 36-41).

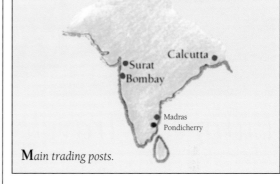

Main trading posts.

A Dutch plantation in India in the seventeenth century.

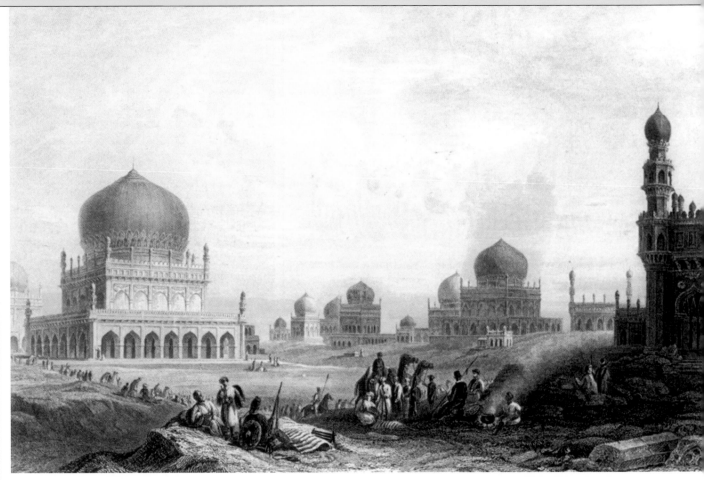

European Travelers

The royal burial place in the fortified city of Golconda. Newbery and Fitch visited this place on their way to Fatehpur Sikri and Akbar s court.

An English traveler in India at about the time of Ralph Fitch's journey.

Ralph Fitch

Ralph Fitch traveled to India in 1583, as one of the first group of English merchants to arrive there to trade. The leader of the group was John Newbery. One of Fitch's duties was the delivery of letters from Queen Elizabeth I to the Emperor Akbar. Newbery and Fitch were arrested in the Persian Gulf by the Portuguese and sent to Goa where they were accused of spying and put in prison. Eventually, they were released on bail and told not to leave Goa. As soon as they could, they fled from the town and escaped. Fitch describes the city as "Golden Goa" because of its wealth.

Newbery and Fitch made their way to Akbar's court at Fatehpur Sikri and delivered the letters from the Queen. On the way to Fatehpur Sikri, they stopped off in Golconda, a city whose exquisite diamonds were world famous. Fitch and Newbery then went their separate ways—Newbery back to England and Fitch eastwards down the Yamuna and Ganges rivers to Bengal. Newbery was never heard of again. Fitch returned to England in 1591.

*M*anucci feeling a patient's pulse. He commissioned this drawing for the front page of the account of his adventures.

Niccolao Manucci

In 1653, aged fourteen, Niccolao Manucci ran away from his home in Venice to go to sea. He reached Surat in 1656, then made his way to Agra.

At this time there was a struggle for power going on between Aurangzeb (see page 31) and his eldest brother, Dara. Manucci joined Dara's army as an **artilleryman.** When Dara was defeated at the Battle of Samugargh, Manucci fled, donned a disguise and joined Aurangzeb's army instead. He later joined up with Dara again and rose to the position of captain of artillery. When Dara was killed by Aurangzeb, Manucci left the army and continued his travels to Delhi, Agra and Bengal.

The Adventures Continue

For the next few years Manucci fought with the Rajputs in the Deccan and made a small fortune (which he lost again) practicing as a doctor, although he had no medical training whatsoever. His lucky break came when he cured one of the royal family of an ear complaint and was appointed official physician. In 1681, however, Manucci left his post and made his way to Goa. His amazing adventures continued. The Portuguese Viceroy sent him on a mission to the Marathas and rewarded him with a knighthood for his efforts. He then served the English governor of Madras as correspondent between the English and Aurangzeb. In return, he was given land and a house in Madras. He died there in 1717.

Shivaji and the Marathas

An English doctor, John Fryer, who traveled to Persia and India from 1672-1681, wrote about the two most remarkable characters of the time— the Great Mughal, Aurangzeb, and his deadly rival, Shivaji, leader of the Hindu Marathas. Shivaji rose from humble origins to become the symbol of Hindu resistance against Aurangzeb's religious intolerance. He was hero-worshiped because of his exploits in battle and his adventures, such as his escape from Aurangzeb's court. Until his death in 1680, Shivaji tricked and outwitted Aurangzeb. His son, Shambuji, was killed by Aurangzeb in 1689. But Shivaji's spirit lived on. In the early twentieth century, his memory was revived to inspire Indians fighting for independence from the British.

A *nineteenth century drawing of Sikh warriors.*

Sikh Religion and Resistance

The Sikh religion was founded in the late fifteenth century by the first Guru (teacher), Guru Nanak. It contained elements of Hinduism and Islam. During the seventeenth century, the Sikhs were persecuted by Aurangzeb and their ninth Guru was murdered in 1675 for refusing to convert to Islam. To protect themselves, the Sikhs formed their own army, called the *Khalsa.* Members of the Khalsa had to wear or carry the five symbols of the Sikh faith. These are the five ks—*kes* (uncut hair), *kangha* (a comb), *kirpan* (a dagger), *kara* (a steel bangle) and *kachh* (breeches or shorts). The Khalsa fought bravely against the Mughals and they succeeded in establishing Sikh rule in the Punjab under Maharaja Ranjit Singh (reigned from 1792-1839).

5 The British Raj 1756-1947

Explorers and Rulers

By 1756, Mughal power was at an end. By the end of the century Maratha power was also over. In their place, the East India Company had been steadily expanding its strength and influence. The Company remained, however, a trading concern, directed by a board and the **shareholders** in London. In 1756-1767, all this changed and the East India Company's attention turned to land and politics. The Company even had its own army to protect its interests. The Company had an important base in Calcutta, Bengal. In 1756, in an effort to regain power, the Nawab (a prince) of Bengal marched into Calcutta and defeated the Company's troops. The British retaliated under the leadership of Robert Clive at the Battle of Plassey in 1757. The Nawab was soundly beaten and the Company effectively became the rulers of Bengal. The victories of Clive over the French East India Company from 1745-61 made the English company's hold over India complete. By the early nineteenth century, it had extended its control over much more of India.

The Battle of Plassey in 1757. The British Lieutenant-Colonel Robert Clive defeated the anti-British ruler of Bengal, Siraj-ud-Daula thus consolidating the East India Company's control over Bengal, the largest province in India.

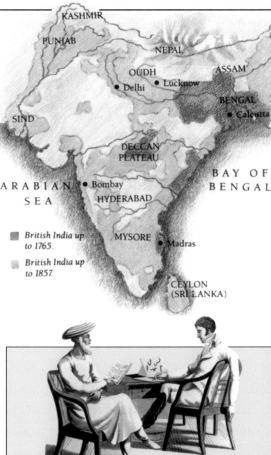

A *European trying to learn Persian from a local teacher, or munshi.*

The Asiatic Society

In 1784, the Asiatic Society of Bengal was founded by Sir William Jones, a British lawyer, judge and **linguist.** Its aim was to encourage the study of Indian languages, literature and culture. Jones had mastered European languages and Turkish, Persian, Arabic and Hebrew. On his arrival in India, he learned Sanskrit so that he could translate ancient Indian texts into English. Jones' work led to a growing interest in Sanskrit literature in Europe and many other scholars of the language joined the Society, such as Thomas Colebrooke (1765-1837) and Dr. Horace Hayman Wilson who became the first Professor of Sanskrit at Oxford University.

The defeat of the Indian forces at Jhansi in 1858.

The Rising of 1857

In 1857, resentment which had been building up amongst Indians against the East India Company and the British came to a head. The army was mostly made up of Indian soldiers, or *sepoys*. They were issued with rifles whose cartridges had to have the tips bitten off before they would fire. Rumors started that the bullets were greased with cow fat (which was unacceptable to Hindus who consider cows sacred) or pig fat (unacceptable to Muslims who consider pigs unclean). The sepoys refused to use the bullets and mutinied. The so-called Indian Mutiny, or First War of Independence, quickly spread across North India. The rebellion had no real leaders and eventually fizzled out after two years. A great deal of anger and suspicion remained on both sides for many years to come.

The Crown Raj

The British government had begun to take a closer interest in the way the East India Company ran their affairs in India. They were not always happy with what they saw and realized that changes needed to be made. In 1858, it was decided that the Company should be abolished and the government of India should pass directly into the hands of the British parliament and crown. A Viceroy (governor) was appointed to represent the crown in India and a Secretary of State for India was appointed in London. In 1876, Queen Victoria was officially proclaimed Empress of India (although she never visited India). Until 1947, India was to remain the "brightest jewel in the **imperial** crown."

British officials conducting part of the survey from the safety of their camp.

The Great Survey of India

As well as being a time of political expansion, the nineteenth century was also a time of geographical exploration. The British Survey of India was begun in 1800, with the aim of producing accurate maps of the country. It was not an easy task! The surveyors' equipment was heavy and cumbersome and there were tigers, snakes, dense jungles and the threat of **malaria** to cope with.

Many of the plants and animals the survey found were shipped back to Britain to be studied at Kew Gardens and London Zoo.

Queen Victoria in 1876, seated on a throne given to her by the Raja of Travancore.

Princes and Politics

Throughout India's history, its kings and princes have played important and colorful parts. Some leaders were famous for their wisdom and courage in battle; others for their fabulous wealth and the splendor of their courts and lifestyles. Many of their palaces can still be seen in India today, although the princes are now princes in name only.

The Princely States

During the time of British Crown rule, India was divided into two parts. About two thirds of the country was governed directly by the British. The rest was made up of about 565 Indian princely states, ruled by maharajas, rajas, nizams and so on. These princes were allowed to keep their titles and their lands, in return for swearing allegiance to the British. Some states, such as Hyderabad, were huge and very wealthy; others were tiny, covering less than a square mile in area (see below left).

Maharaja Dulep Singh painted in the 1850s.

Some of the six hundred princely states of India. The states were too scattered to form a threat to the British Raj. They were finally abolished by the leaders of independent India in 1971.

The beautiful Lake Palace in Udaipur, Rajasthan. Built by Maharaja Jagat Singh II in 1754. It is now used as a luxury hotel.

Ranjit Singh –
the Lion of Punjab

The Sikh kingdom of the Punjab (see map on page 38) was one of the last regions of India to come under British control. Maharaja Ranjit Singh, known as the Lion of Punjab, ruled his kingdom shrewdly and bravely from 1792 to his death in 1839.

Although he was a Sikh, he sought the advice of many Hindus and Muslims who lived in

Ranjit Singh, ruler of Punjab

Punjab and managed to maintain religious harmony in his kingdom. The British could not overpower Ranjit Singh. Instead they were forced to sign treaties of "perpetual friendship" with him. Ranjit Singh was a vital part of British plans to take over Afghanistan, and had to be kept on their side. With his help, the British succeeded in getting rid of the Afghan king, Dost Muhammed, and replacing him with a weak ruler, Shah Shuja, who would act on behalf of the British. The result was disastrous, however. The Afghans rebelled and returned Dost Muhammed to his throne.

When Ranjit Singh died no strong ruler took his place. After two Sikh Wars in 1845-46 and 1849, the Punjab also came under British control.

British officers being entertained at the court of an Indian prince in 1820.

The City Palace in Jaipur, home of the Maharajas of Jaipur since the early eighteenth century.

Treasure and Poverty

Many of the larger princely states were famous for their legendary wealth. Some princes lived in great luxury, eating off golden plates and wearing clothes of gold and silver thread. The last Nizam of Hyderabad was reported to be one of the world's richest men. There were jewels everywhere in his palace, including emeralds the size of eggs and buckets and buckets of pearls. The royal family of Baroda owned a pearl necklace, with pearls as big as marbles, and jewelry said to have belonged to **Napoleon Bonaparte.** The Maharaja of Jaipur's treasure was so well guarded that the Maharaja himself had difficulty in being allowed to see it.

But there was another side to India – that of poverty. The majority of people living in India were very poor due to harsh systems of local taxation and famine. The combination of droughts, floods and badly **irrigated** land sometimes caused appalling shortages of food.

From finery to famine—victims of the Madras famine in 1878.

Life in the Raj

Ncw British arrivals in Bombay in 1916.

Fanny Bullock Workman dressed for mountain climbing.

Women Travelers

Most of the women who went to India rarely traveled, if they could help it. But a few were more adventurous. An American, Fanny Bullock Workman, became famous for her cycle rides and mountaineering. In 1898, she and her husband cycled from Cape Comorin all the way north to Peshawar and the Himalayas. She wrote down details of every building they passed but was much less interested in the people of India. Between 1898-1912, she climbed many of the highest Himalayan peaks.

The heyday of the British Raj from 1858-1905 saw a great influx of people from Britain in search of jobs in the government, **civil service** or army. Many were fairly well off already; others came to seek their fortunes. They sailed from England on one of the great ocean liners, down the Suez Canal to Aden, then across the Indian Ocean. On reaching the Suez Canal, passengers were allowed to change into their tropical dress. The journey lasted several months, giving them plenty of time to prepare for the culture shock ahead. They also had time to read the many helpful pamphlets available, such as *How to Pack, How to Dress, How to Keep Well on a Winter Tour of India (for Ladies)* and *Notes for Officers Proceeding to India.*

During the Raj, the British had thousands of miles of railway track laid all over India. This enabled more Indians to travel and make pilgrimages, and for **nationalist** feelings to be communicated throughout the country. This photograph was taken by Colonel Yule in 1863. British officers were encouraged to take photographs and these proved to be invaluable aids to scholars, surveyors, the government and the army.

Hunting and shooting were popular among British officers and Indian princes alike.

Arrival in India

In India itself, British society was divided into a rigid order. At the top of the scale came the senior government officials and civil servants; below them came army officers, then business people, then ordinary soldiers and then Indians. In the seventeenth and eighteenth centuries, employees of the East India Company had often married Indian women but, by the nineteenth century, this was frowned upon. Most British people kept themselves separate from the Indians, apart from upper-class Indians such as the princes. Many considered the Indians to be inferior to them. Most of the British felt they had a duty to rule India, but not to get involved with the people or culture of the country.

Business as Usual

Many British people in India tried to carry on their lives pretty much as they would have at home. They brought their servants, furniture, clothes (often unsuitable for a hot climate) and even pets with them. They had English food and wine sent over from home. Once in India, they surrounded themselves with a household of Indian servants—cooks, fan-pullers, ayahs (nannies) and so on. While their husbands were out at work, the women had plenty of time on their hands. They painted, wrote letters home, went to church, organized balls, garden parties and amateur dramatics to fill in their days. Among the men, polo, hunting, badminton and going to their clubs were favorite leisure activities. In the hot season, people escaped to the cool of the hill stations, such as Simla in Himachal Pradesh.

A *Christian missionary in India.*

Missionary Fever

In 1813, the ban on British missionaries travelling to India and settling there was lifted, although the British still weren't keen on missionaries until the 1830s-40s. A wave of missionaries set sail in the hope of converting India's "benighted **heathens**" to Christianity. Despite their best efforts, very few Indians became Christians. Quite a large number of the converts were low-caste Hindus or poor Muslims who looked to Christianity as a means of escape. There were some notable pioneer British missionaries such as William Carey who translated the Bible into Indian languages and Alexander Duff who helped to shape the educational system of India through missionary schools for the working classes.

6 Modern India

Towards Independence

Towards the end of the nineteenth century, a new, **nationalist** reform movement began to take hold in India. It was led by a group of young, wealthy, educated Indians who believed that Indians should be in charge of their own country and that it was time for the British to go.

The Indian National Congress and Muslim League

The Indian National Congress was founded in 1885 as a political party dedicated to getting the views of Indians heard in government. Gradually, self-rule for India became its aim. Among its founders and first presidents were Mahadev G. Ranade (1842-1901) and Gopal K. Gokhale (1866-1915). Both taught that it was time for India to reform and stand on its own two feet. They were joined by the more radical Bal G. Tilak (1856-1920) who believed that India needed to be free first, before it tackled reform.

Congress was a mainly Hindu movement and, in 1906, the Muslim League was founded by Aga Khan. The league was initially a pro-British organization but with the election of Mohammad Ali Jinnah to its leadership, home-rule, and eventually the establishment of the state of Pakistan became its aim.

A *Muslim League rally demanding a separate Muslim state within or apart from India.*

Mahatma Gandhi with Sarojini Naidu the first Indian woman to be elected President of Congress in 1925.

Mahatma Gandhi

One of the most important and influential figures in the Indian independence movement was a lawyer, Mohandas K. Gandhi (1869-1948). Gandhi spent twenty years in South Africa where he worked to try and lessen the discrimination shown towards Indians. He returned to India in 1915. Gandhi worked with the Congress but he also spread the message of independence to the mass of India's population by visiting thousands of countryside villages over a period of many years. He became known as Mahatma which means Great Soul.

The British failed to keep their promises of a greater share of power for Indians and they also ignored the contribution made by Indians who fought in the First World War. The final straw came in 1919 when the British massacred four hundred Indians at **Jallianwala Bagh.** Gandhi urged people to follow his policy of non-violent, passive resistance. He also encouraged them to stop buying British-made cloth and to spin their own instead.

In his book, The Discovery of India, Nehru explored his own ideas of what sort of country India was and how it might develop.

Independence and Partition

After World War II, it became obvious that the British could not justify their presence in India for very much longer. The "Quit India" campaign gained momentum. In 1947, the British government appointed Lord Mountbatten as the viceroy who would preside over India's independence. India became an independent country on August 15, 1947, with Jawaharlal Nehru, Gandhi's greatest follower, as its first prime minister. But there was a price to pay for freedom. The Muslim League had been campaigning for a separate Muslim country, Pakistan, which would include part of Punjab in the west and Bengal in the east. Millions of people were forced to leave their homes and millions more were killed in the violence that followed. This is known as the "partition" of India. Gandhi also became a victim of the Hindu-Muslim rivalry. In January 1948, he was shot dead by a Hindu fanatic who resented his concern for the Muslims. Nehru remained as Prime Minister until his death in 1964.

Lord Mountbatten, India's last Viceroy, being greeted by people shortly after the announcement of India's independence.

Hindu-Muslim rivalry erupted in violence and rioting in the major Indian cities. These were the scenes in the streets of Bombay in 1946.

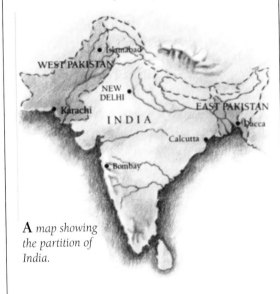

A map showing the partition of India.

India Today

India is the world's largest democracy. It has never come under military rule, unlike its neighbors, despite having the world's fourth largest army. In recent years India has seen the assassination of two prime ministers, Hindu-Muslim riots and corruption scandals among politicians.

Relations with Pakistan remain tense. At partition in 1947 the Hindu ruler of Kashmir opted to join India, although most Kashmiris are Muslim. Kashmir was divided up and there have been disputes over its ownership ever since, resulting in border wars with Pakistan in 1948 and 1965 and continual outbreaks of fighting there. In 1971 India's armed forces intervened to support East Pakistan in its breakaway to become independent as Bangladesh. Cross-border terrorism in Kashmir and in India itself remains a big problem. The worst violence of recent years was a terrorist attack in Mumbai that killed more than 200 people.

Progress and Problems

Economic and social progress have been uneven. India can manufacture tanks, fighter planes and missiles and in 1998 became a nuclear power. Bangalore is a worldclass center of computer expertise. India is home to the world's largest film industry. Foreign tourists flock to the beaches of Goa and to see the glories of Mughal architecture in Delhi and Agra. There are nearly 700 universities but, although there is now a primary school in every village, more than 280 million Indian adults are still illiterate. The transport and power systems struggle to keep up with the demands made on them.

Despite birth control programs, population continues to rise, with a population of more than 1 billion by 2015. India may one day overtake China to become the world's most populous nation. As a result, tens of millions are unemployed, with many forced into begging or crime to survive. In the countryside the rising number of people seeking land to cultivate and fuel to burn has made deforestation a major problem. Natural disasters are made worse by the crowded conditions, too.

Technological achievements include solar power plants and an advanced space program.

A cooking pot shop in Jaipur, Rajasthan.

The countryside in Goa

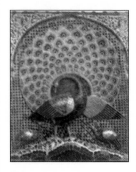

Traditional crafts

The Calcutta Stock Exchange.

Handmade pottery bein sold in the street.

Indian children.

The elephant-headed Hindu god, Ganesh.

The New Explorers

Despite its problems, India continues to exert its magic and and fascination over people. In the 1960s, the new invaders were hippies from Europe who came to India in search of spiritual enlightenment! Today, thousands of tourists visit India to explore its sights and the glories of its checkered past—the Taj Mahal of the Mughals, the palaces of the rajas and maharajas and the Victorian stately homes of the British. Alongside these are the particularly Indian sights, sounds, smells and experiences which have lasted through thousands of years of visitors, invaders and explorers.

Blue houses in Jodhpur, Rajasthan.

Modern-day India covers some 1.24 million square miles (3.3 million sq km) and is divided into 26 states and several **union territories**. More than 1.2 billion people live in India, making it the second most populous country in the world behind China. Hindi, English, and 22 regional languages, together with hundreds of local languages and dialects are spoken in India.

India Timeline

c.5000 BCE	Farming has begun in western parts of India.
c.2500 BCE	The Indus Valley Civilization is at its height.
c.1500 BCE	The Aryans invade from the northwest. Their Vedic religion forms the basis of Hinduism.
326 BCE	Alexander of Macedonia (Greece) crosses the River Indus into India.
50 CE	Trade flourishes between India and the Roman Empire.
c.320-550	The Gupta Empire and the golden age of Hinduism in India.
630-645	The Chinese Buddhist monk, Hsuan Tsang, visits India.
1206	The Muslim Sultanate of Delhi is established in North India.
1498	The Portuguese (led by Vasco da Gama) arrive in India.
1526	The founding of the Mughal Empire in India.
1619	The English East India Company set up their first factory at Surat.
1632	Shah Jahan begins building the Taj Mahal, in memory of his wife.
1720	The French establish a trading post at Pondicherry near Madras.
1784	The India Act. The British take political control of India.
1792-1839	Ranjit Singh rules over the Sikh kingdom of Punjab.
1857	The First War of Independence (also called the Indian Mutiny).
1876	Queen Victoria is proclaimed Empress of India.
1920	Mahatma Gandhi launches his campaign of civil disobedience.
1947	India gains independence.
1948	Gandhi is assassinated.
1962	Indo-China War.
1964	Jawaharlal Nehru, India's first Prime Minister dies.
1966	Nehru's daughter, Indira Gandhi, becomes Prime Minister.
1971	India-Pakistan War.
1984	Mrs Gandhi is assassinated. Her son, Rajiv, takes over.
1991	Prime Minister Rajiv Gandhi assassinated.
1992	Hindu–Muslim riots kill 1,200.
1997	India celebrates 50 years of independence.
2002	India threatens war with Pakistan over its alleged support for cross-border terrorism
2007	Pratibha Patil becomes first female India president.
2008	Terrorist attackes in Mumbai result in more than 200 deaths.
2008	India launches first mission to moon.
2014	India holds the largest democratic election in history, as more than 550 million people go to the polls, where they choose Narendra Modi as prime minister.
2015	A 7.9 earthquake in Nepal destroys buildings in northern India.

Glossary

archaeologist: a person who studies the past by methodically **excavating** ancient sites and **artifacts.**

artifact: an ancient object.

artilleryman: a soldier who operates guns and cannon.

banyan: a tropical tree whose roots grow above ground before they reach down into the soil.

bartering: goods that are exchanged for other goods are bartered.

batik: a way of making a pattern on cloth with wax. The wax design is applied to the cloth, which is then dipped in dye.

chronicler: someone who writes down an account of a person's life.

citadel: a fortress, often built on top of a hill overlooking a city.

civil service: the administrative staff who carry out the orders of the government.

Commonwealth: an organization of states who were once (or still are) ruled by Great Britain.

delta: the area at the mouth of a large river where the river meets the sea and drops its load of sediment.

deported: exiled, banished or sent away from a country.

dialogue: a piece of writing in the form of a conversation.

Durga: a warrior-like Hindu goddess, shown riding on a tiger and carrying various weapons in her ten arms.

enlightened: to have seen the light, or the truth of the matter.

envoy: a messenger or representative of a king or queen.

excavated: dug up in a methodical and scientific manner.

funeral pyre: a large pile of wood on which a dead body is cremated (burnt).

heathen: the name given by followers of some religions to people who do not share their particular beliefs.

imperial: when one country politically or economically dominates another (or many countries) it is described as imperialist.

indigo: a dye made from vegetable matter that has a violet-blue color.

Indo-European: the people and group of languages which originally came from the region between and including India and Europe.

irrigate: to water an area of land by a system of canals or waterways.

Jallianwala Bagh: a massacre of Indians by soldiers under British control on April 13, 1919 in Amritsar. The army opened fire on people who had assembled for a Hindu festival in a walled garden.

Jesuit: a member of the Roman Catholic Order of Jesus, founded by St Ignatius in the sixteenth century CE.

Kublai Khan: (c.1215-1294), ruler of China and Mongolia, and grandson of Genghis Khan.

linguist: someone who speaks or writes a variety of languages.

litter: a chair carried by servants.

malaria: a disease spread by mosquitoes in tropical Asia and Africa. Symptoms include high fever, then severe chills. Malaria can be fatal and can recur.

Mesopotamia: the area between the Euphrates and Tigris rivers (modern-day Iraq). In Mesopotamia the civilizations of Sumer and Babylon thrived.

middlemen: a merchant who buys goods from the producer and then sells the same goods on to the trader who will in turn sell them to the consumer.

missionary: someone who tries to convert people from one religion to another.

monsoon: seasonal winds which occur in Asia. They blow from the southwest in summer bringing heavy rains, and from the northeast in winter.

mosque: a place of worship for Muslims.

muslin: a very fine cloth made out of cotton that looks like gauze.

Napoleon Bonaparte: (1769-1821), a general who made himself the French Emperor after his success in the French Revolutionary Wars.

nationalist: someone who is devoted to their country and believes in its independence.

Old Silk Road: the route or routes used by merchants carrying silk westwards from China.

opulent: very rich or wealthy.

orientalist: one who studies the cultures and languages of the East.

Parsi: a follower of Zoroastrianism, a religion which spread from Iran to India in the seventh century CE.

patronage: financial support and encouragement given by someone such as a king to favored artists.

pilgrimage: a journey, made as an act of religious devotion, to a sacred place.

proclamation: a public announcement made about important affairs of state.

reincarnation: the belief that, when you die, you are reborn into another life.

relic: anything that once belonged to saint or religious figure.

religious tolerance: recognition and acceptance of other people's beliefs.

republic: an independent country which has no monarch and is ruled by an elected government.

revival: a renewal of interest in something such as art or literature.

Sanskrit: the ancient language of India, which has special importance as the sacred language of the Hindu holy books.

shareholders: people who own shares in a company. A share is a certain percentage of the wealth of the company. The company is expected to generate profits to increase the investment that the shareholder has made.

Slave Dynasty: the Muslim rulers of North India from 1206-1290. The dynasty was so-called because several of its most important rulers were ex-slaves.

Swami: the title given to a Hindu religious teacher.

tortoiseshell: the shell of sea turtles.

union territory: a region, such as a large island or city, which is part of India but does not count as a separate state.

Index

Numbers in **bold** indicate an illustration. Words in **bold** are in the glossary on page 47.

Photographic credits

Cover: Main: Javarman/Dreamstimes.com; Gandhi: Wikimedia; statue: Elesi/Dollar Photo.
Interior: The Ancient Art and Architecture Collection 9 bottom, 11 top, 35 right; Archiv fur Kunst und Geschichte, Berlin 27 bottom, 38 top; The Bridgeman Art Library 5, 9 top 20, 28 bottom left by Courtesy of the Board of Trustees of the V & A and top right, 29 top left Bodleian Library, 30 top right and bottom left, 34 bottom; C M Dixon 15 top; E.T. Archive 32 bottom, 41 bottom; Mary Evans Picture Library 19 bottom 23, 26 right, 30 top left, 31 top right, 34 top, 39 top left, 40 top left; Giraudon/The Bridgeman Art Library 22, Sonia Halliday Photographs 19 top, 21 right; Hansmann 11 bottom Robert Harding Picture Library 7 middle and bottom, 8, 10, 13 bottom, 14, 15 bottom, 17, 21 left, 22/23 Bodleian Library, 25 bottom, 26 left British Museum, 29 top right Freer Gallery of Art, Washington, 32 top, 35 left Bibliotheque Nationale, 39 bottom left; Hulton Deutsch Collection Limited 36 right, 37 top left and bottom, 40 top right, 42 top, 43 top right; The Hutchison Library 3, 44 top right; Vanessa Kelly 30 middle right, 31 top left and bottom right, 38 bottom, 39 top right, 44 bottom center left, bottom left and bottom right, 45 left; The Mansel Collection 2, 7 top, 36 bottom middle, 41 top; The National Trust Photographic Library 36 bottom left; Andrew Oliver title page, 27 top, 28 top left and top middle, 28/29, 31 bottom left 44 top center left and center right, 45 right; Popperfoto 42 bottom, 43 bottom; Royal Geographical Society Picture Library 25 top, 39 bottom right 40 bottom; Syndication International 12, 13 top, 33 top Pierpoint Morgan Library and bottom; Rijksmuseum, Amsterdam 37 top right; India Office Library 43 top left.